Never Mind a Million

© 2023 Richard Gentle. All rights reserved.

ISBN 978-1-8383550-4-3

© Cover Design Richard Gentle

Keekoo Publications

First Published in 2023

www.keekoo.co.uk

Contents

Introduction 1
A focus on money 2
Why do I really want more money? 3
Why can't I win millions? 5
Taking responsibility 6
Beware of the big statements 8
Get rich quick schemes (GRQS) 9
Gambling 10
Loan sharks 10
Credit cards, bank loans, and store cards 11
Starting points 13
The psychology of taking small actions 16
Where you live and who you know 20
Set a realistic goal or target 21
Ask yourself questions before making purchases 22
Do not resent paying your bills 23
Why do we buy things? 25
The false optimism of sudden financial improvement 25
Equality versus equal opportunity 28
The difference between 'haves' and 'have-nots' 30
Never a lender or a borrower be 32
Passive income 32
Selling your service and deciding on cost 36
Further techniques 38

The funnel of money ... 38
A deep dive into metaphysics ... 40
Brain and Mind ... 40
A two-way highway ... 44
Back to money and finances ... 47
The choice to feel different ... 52
Do not check for change ... 53
You live in a physical reality – give it time ... 55
New Habits ... 56
Intention ... 61
Expectation ... 62
The magical approach ... 62
Surrender ... 64
And then it was gone ... 65

Introduction

At a time when many people are struggling to make ends meet, financially, it's also noticeable that people are taking the wrong approach to improving their situation because they do not understand where, or how, to focus their attention. It seems that the more we struggle, or the harder we work, the poorer we become.

Since you are reading this booklet, it's likely you are either having some measure of financial difficulty, or you wish to improve your financial experience. Furthermore, you may have thought: "If only I could win the Lottery." But here's the point; if you are used to managing on a low income, you are probably not used to having a large amount of money – unless perhaps, you had previously experienced having a large amount of money. There are always exceptions and some people do go from 'rags to riches,' or from wealth to poverty, overnight. But, for the majority of people, this is not the case.

This booklet aims to offer you a mixture of insights and techniques that could help you to change your perception of money and bring more of it into your life. It's also written to take into account a variety of ideas: some conventionally logical, rational, and mainstream; others connected to psychology; and quite a few based around metaphysical knowledge.

Before we begin, a note on terms and grammar
In this book, I write both 'your self' and 'yourself'. This is deliberate to place emphasis on your individual personal selfhood, or to say 'yourself,' in general passing terms. UK readers may also notice that I often use 'that' instead of 'which,' taking account of the now more common usage beyond our shores. I also deliberately use 'they' and 'their' when grammatically, in a traditional sense, it should sometimes be 'his/her' – but this reflects the way most people now speak, and how some feel about gender identity. It is also less clumsy to read.

A focus on money

Sometimes, when you are outside of a culture, you notice things that natives of that culture may no longer see, appreciate, or simply ignore. For many years, as an indigenous Brit based in the UK, it has often struck me that many people tend to use money as their main motivator for getting others involved with anything. Promises of wealth seem to head the table of reasons to be alive. Now I'm not saying that we Brits are exempt from this attitude and indeed, here in the UK we tend to follow many of the social trends established by those countries we often admire. It's always been a standing joke that Brits spend all their time talking about the weather, but certainly over recent years, conversation around money has somewhat overtaken this. Many of what have been termed, 'the developing nations' have also concluded that having money is a key component of succeeding in most endeavours – and escaping from seemingly impoverished situations. It would appear that people with money are generally perceived as being happier and more successful; live abundant lifestyles; are able to do more exciting activities; and have more toys to play with. But the obsession with focusing on money, rather than focusing on happiness and personal fulfilment, is causing a lot of heartache and disappointment around the world – not to mention the destruction of natural resources to gain every last penny possible. We have become so obsessed with striving for money that many of us fail to ask an important question:

Why do I really want more money?

Many people say they want more money – in fact, large amounts of money. But have you honestly asked yourself: "Why do *I* want more money?" Have you ever made a list of things you need money for? Let's consider a few beliefs around possible reasons for wanting more money:

- Money enables you to make more choices in life.

- There are specific things you need specific amounts of money for.
- You want a better quality of life.
- You want to be seen as successful.
- You want people to respect you.
- You want more leisure time.
- You want to be able to do more things in your life.
- You want to experience what it feels like to have more abundance.
- You want to be in control and not controlled by other people.
- You want to be able to help other people – family and friends.
- You don't want to be a slave to hard work.
- You don't really want to work at all – well not in conventional ways.
- You want to contribute financially to a community or to a good cause.

You can make your own list but, looking through the items above, do you notice anything about some of the desires? Most are quite vague. Let's take for example, 'wanting to do more things in life.' What things do you want to do more of? You may be so caught up in surviving, that you haven't actually thought very deeply about the things you'd like to do. It's a bit like a person who works hard all of their life, who keeps saying: "When I retire, I'll have time to do all the things I want to do." Again... what things?

For many years of my past life, living independently from parents, many of my waking thoughts consisted of: 'How will I pay for such and such, by such and such a date?' There was little time to think: 'What will I enjoy doing today, tomorrow, later in the week, this year?' When I eventually became completely debt free, my question went from, 'how can I survive another week?' to 'what do I want to do with my life now?' If only I had spent a bit more time on the second question and less on worrying about the first – perhaps I would have got to where I am now, much quicker. With all this in mind, another question arises:

Why can't I win millions?

Here are just a few possible reasons why you may not be able to attract big money:

- You don't actually buy a lottery ticket or enter competitions for money.
- You do not believe it is really possible to gain 'big money'.
- You are used to living in a state of lack that you are still focused on.
- You have developed 'poverty consciousness' – believing you will always struggle.
- Money has always been a problem for you.
- You worry that you may not be worthy to receive more.

- The word 'money' brings up negative connotations and emotions.
- You resent people who have a lot of money.
- You believe that people with more money than they need are selfish.
- You believe that you cannot have money and still be spiritual or creative.
- You believe that some people with incredible wealth must have got it dishonestly.
- You judge value according to others' apparent monetary wealth.
- You feel that life has dealt you a 'bad hand'.
- It's just down to good or bad luck, why some people get more than others.
- You believe that you are a victim of circumstances beyond your control.
- You believe that the only ways to get money are through hard work, winning money, having friends or relatives that will help you, or receiving any available State benefits.
- You keep reinforcing your lack when you look at what you don't have.

Taking responsibility

The first thing you must do is accept 100% responsibility for your life and its circumstances. I'm not saying you should interpret this in a personal blame way, like: "It's all my fault." or in a way that implies current fate or fixed future destiny. What it means is that you have the power to change your circumstances and to improve your current situation. Accepting full responsibility is very empowering. You may have got yourself into this situation, but you also have the ability to get yourself out of it – no matter how overwhelming it may seem in this moment.

Many of us live in consumer societies where material gain and wealth is the mark of value and worthiness. We compare where we are in relation to where everyone else is. Perhaps this would be a good time to point out, in these terms: Yes, there are always people better off than you, but there are always people worse off than you. That should make you feel a bit better. Either way, you are not alone.

Like most established professions, psychology likes its labels and has often described personality types as, 'glass half empty' or 'glass half full'. If you are honest, you probably already know which you are – at least at the moment. But if you admit to being the former, you can still change into the latter. When you encounter a problem, do you think, "how can I make this problem go away?" or do you think, "I wonder what solution I could come up with to experience a better situation?" The difference in thinking may seem subtle, but there is a difference, and it's having a 'solution focused mindset'.

"You cannot turn your attention to a problem without shining your attention on it, activating the vibration within you. Every thought is already vibrating, so when you focus on it you activate the vibration of it within you. – Abraham[1]

In other words, you make the problem more prominent in your mind, when you think about it and have an associated emotional response.

Beware of the big statements

How many times have you heard people say: "I was down and out and within only a month of [put here whatever change, course, or training you've heard mentioned] I made $100,000. The tendency is to feel overwhelmed. For most people, such numbers are out of the range of their comprehension – whether through work or winning potential. However, if the same person had said: "I was down and out and suddenly, I was given $10." you probably wouldn't take much notice. But very often, this is where you're at; this could be your starting point. Furthermore, we all have different personalities and some people find it easier to take the sort of action seemingly required to make money, more than others – but you can retrain your mind to change this. And of course, when you can already do something with ease, you often

---

[1] Abraham (A channelled 'collective' of non-physical beings, "interpreted" by Esther Hicks)

cannot understand why others cannot do it too. But if all of us could do everything, there wouldn't be anything left to learn about, or discover.

Get rich quick schemes (GRQS)

I'm sure you've come across them; perhaps you've even tried a few. I know I have in the past – albeit briefly. The times when these schemes are most often turned to, are when someone has reached a point of desperation in their financial health. However, there are a few things you probably need to know – if you haven't already realised:

1. By the time you come across a GRQS, it's probably already too late to make much from it. The traditional and most notorious schemes were labelled 'pyramid selling,' and later made illegal in many countries. Despite this, some GRQS still have the qualities of pyramid selling – sometimes refined as 'multi-level marketing.' Essentially, it's all about recruiting others into a scheme with the originator at the top receiving payments in varying amounts from all those below. One of the main issues people experience with this sort of scheme, is not being able to find enough people willing to find more people, to keep the scheme going. In some schemes, it's a bit like a 'chain letter.' It relies on no one breaking the link.

2. Getting something for nothing. The saying accompanying this is often: 'There's no such thing as a free lunch.'
3. Finding a great bargain. The saying accompanying this is often: 'Buyer beware.'

Consider the above when you come across anything that seems 'too good to be true.' Ask yourself if it falls into one of the above mentioned categories.

Gambling

It might seem obvious that for most of us, gambling is not a good idea. The saying accompanying this is often: 'Only pay out what you can afford to lose.' Lots of people have an occasional 'flutter' with gambling, but there are many who find it addictive and get into serious trouble. I once knew a lad who got caught up with gambling, and witnessing his obsessive addiction was actually quite scary to be around.

Loan sharks

These are unregulated people who offer to lend varying sums of money. The catch is that they demand a high interest on their return payments, are unregulated, and can even threaten violence against your non-repayment. They can be friends, acquaintances, or people recommended by others – either through other people you may know, or through some form of media advertising.

Credit cards, bank loans, and store cards

I've lumped together this next lot, because essentially they are deemed legitimate and legally regulated sources of extra money. Surprisingly perhaps, many people who take up one of these options do not understand the term APR. This is 'Annual Percentage Rate' and refers to the yearly interest charged to borrowers. The calculations can be quite complex, but the main thing to appreciate is that the higher the number, the more you will be repaying above the original amount borrowed. Furthermore, you will find that when you get into credit cards, your monthly repayment will never quite be fully paid off – even when you think you're repaying the outstanding balance in full. Admittedly, you can get deals that are 'interest free' for a period of time, but once these end, interest is applied and carried forward on the amount borrowed. There is also something known as 'compound interest.' This is the interest earned on the interest. This can be good when you are a saver (albeit reliant on the general economic climate), but not good when you are a borrower. Lastly, store cards which offer 'buy now, pay later' credit cards, or in-house loan agreements, often carry a higher APR than regular bank credit cards. They may entice you with additional percentages off purchases, or free gifts, but ultimately, they will most likely cost you more than simply using a bank's credit card or loan facilities.

The main entrapment of credit cards is that you soon reach your limit and can no longer pay off the outstanding amount in full each month. You then find yourself repaying only the monthly interest, calculated over the whole of the amount outstanding. At this point, some people transfer to another credit card with a new interest free period, and some people take out a loan to pay off the credit card – this is because the interest on a loan is usually less than it would be if you kept paying the interest on a card. Whichever situation you find yourself in, consider this:

Getting another credit card or a loan does not mean you now have more money

I've always been amazed by not only commercial advertising promoting loans of any amount, but also by people who call themselves advisers, who should know better. Short term loans, based on the idea that you'll soon be in a better position to manage your finances, rarely work out well. A few people may get additional work and income but, for most, their circumstances will be the same again next month. Now you have the same amount of money going out, plus the monthly repayment on what you borrowed to initially alleviate the first shortfall. Always ask yourself:

If I borrow today, will I have enough money next time?

You have to cover what you have borrowed, on top of your usual outgoings.

Starting points

From a rational perspective, it's helpful to know where you stand financially, right now. This means knowing what income and outgoings you have. You need to be honest with yourself. I've known of people who leave bills unopened, or who absolutely refuse to look at their bank balances – never mind their monthly statements. However, once you know your current position, it's much easier to take some action in a meaningful and positive direction.

There are a few relatively simple things you can start doing that could turn your fortunes around. Let's start with some rational, logical steps:

1. Add up all your weekly or monthly outgoings and see how this matches all of your incomings.
2. See if you have any regular outgoing payments that you could cancel. These could

be subscriptions to things you could do without or services you rarely use or no longer need.
3. List your regular priority payments. These could typically be rent or mortgage; local or other government taxes; home energy costs; food.
4. List any other regular payments you make.
5. Think about some of your casual purchases that you could probably manage without.

Following our rational approach, if you are already in debt, or debt is beginning to run away with you, contact any of your creditors to see if there's any help available, or an option whereby you could stop paying the usual amounts for a fixed period of time, to give you a breathing space. In the past, people were often terrified by the idea of having to talk to the people they owed money to, but times have moved on and industry regulated creditors would generally prefer to help you to pay something, rather than everything suddenly going quiet and then receiving nothing at all. In many instances, your accounts can be frozen and debts can be made interest-free so that you stop paying further cumulative interest. This may, but not necessarily, affect your credit rating – but if you are in financial trouble, a good credit rating won't do much for you anyway. Oddly, borrowing to increase your debt, but always making regular monthly repayments, can give you the best credit rating available – you're reliable and your creditors are profiting from you! In the past, I have come across people who have wondered why their credit rating isn't as good as they'd expected: They'd never got into debt, never borrowed, and maybe even had good working incomes, but this also meant there was no track record of borrowing and paying back on time, etc.

There are often a number of options available. You can manage things with your creditors by yourself, or you can enter into more official avenues of help. In the UK we have an independent 'Citizens Advice' organisation and they can make an initial assessment of your situation and then offer to contact creditors on your behalf. There are a number of pathways you could explore: One is an Individual Voluntary Arrangement (IVA). This is a legal agreement that looks at your available income after all priority bills have been taken into account and determines, with agreement from the creditors involved, how much you can pay back each one, weekly or monthly. Once set up, these often have a finite duration of around five to six years, after which, as long as you have made consistent repayments, any remaining debt is effectively written off.

In my own case, as the years went by managing things myself, my debts started being sold to other agencies and periodically, I'd receive settlement offers below the value of the outstanding balances. It was in fact, this very situation that eventually enabled me to clear my debts to a level of satisfaction (actually, they call it 'unsatisfied') and this meant the debt was officially ended and any future action was terminated.

Options do, of course, change and seeking advice on the Internet, or in person with various professional organisations, can provide you with a clearer idea of what may be available, or whether you actually want to pursue this type of action. Other countries may have similar organisations that offer help.

The psychology of taking small actions

Having explored some recognised conventional approaches, we now create a bridge to metaphysics, via some rational psychology. The first point was recommended to me by a friend:

- Leave some money on a table where you'll see it every day. This should be paper money and not coins as, psychologically, paper money feels of greater value. Place a little note next to the money: 'I am wealthy.' You are not going to use this money. Instead, use other money you have for buying things. Each time you see the money lying there, you are going to think to yourself: "I am so wealthy, I don't need to use that money." After a short while, you will add to this

money and sometimes, you may be surprised when other people see it and add to it, too.
- If you go to a bargain or charity/thrift store, do not go because you feel poor; go because it is fun to find something exciting. Already you are putting yourself in a different mindset. The same goes for reduced cost food aisles.
- If you see two items, but one is better quality or makes you feel better than the other, buy the better item if you can – particularly if it's only slightly more expensive.
- Imagine how you would feel if you had plenty of money. How would you behave? How would you think? How would you dress? How would you walk? Where would you go? What would you do? What would you eat and drink? What would you talk about? Try to do this exercise daily, with focused concentration for at least 68 seconds.[2]
- Be aware of what you say to other people, whether family, friends, or work colleagues. Avoid talking about how hard things are, or tough times. If you do find yourself getting caught up in such conversations, pick the role of the person who says something positive, even if you at first have to acknowledge another person's negativity –

---

[2] Abraham suggests that 'law of attraction' starts to kick in at 17 seconds of focused thought. By the time you reach 68 seconds, this is equivalent to 2 million physical action hours of activity.

or change the subject to something more uplifting.
- Be aware of what you say to your self – often termed 'self-talk'. If you catch yourself being negative about 'your self', try to immediately counteract the negative for something more positive: "I cancel that negative thought – I'm actually amazing." Think of anything that you have achieved or mastered.
- When you see something you want, do not say, "I can't afford that." Instead say: "I could have that, but I will wait and choose something better."
- If you are in a lot of debt and have managed to freeze any action against you (see paragraphs above this section) and you are paying a fixed amount back each month, change the way you view your situation. Imagine you have a cheap-to-repay loan, rather than an unmanageable debt. This can be a helpful psychological step – same money outstanding, but a different and more positive perspective.
- Hold the intention that you will pay outstanding bills and any debts you have accrued. This does not mean you have to pay everything immediately or even that you can pay anything at all; it's simply having the intention – again, making sure you develop a healthy mindset.
- Imagine how it might feel if you had no debts... but imagine in terms of having

abundance. Bashar[3] defines true abundance as: *"Being able to do what you need to do, when you need to do it."*

- If you find that certain words, such as 'money' cause a negative emotion inside you, pick more friendly words that help you to feel better. Likewise, if you associate the word 'work' with feelings of stress, and cannot see how you can have one without the other, choose a different association. Personally, I decided to think in terms of: "My enjoyable activities produce many varied income streams."

Here is a similar idea to the first one, mentioned above, from Heidi M:[4]

"Carry a $100 dollar bill in your pocket. Every time you put your hand in your pocket you will touch it and remember how rich you are."

Remember, it does not matter how much comes to you. Dr Wayne Dyer once said:

"Every time I see a coin on the street, I stop, pick it up, put it into my pocket, and say out loud, "Thank you God for this symbol of abundance that keeps flowing into my life." Never once have I asked,

---

[3] Bashar – an alien personality channelled by Darryl Anka
[4] Attendee at Andy Dooley's 'The Manifestors Cafe'

"Why only a penny, God? You know I need a lot more than that."[5]

Where you live and who you know

I've often said: 'If you want to understand your state of wellbeing, look around you at your environment and also think about the people you spend most time with. Indeed, it has been said that, 'you are the average of the five people you spend the most time with' and further to this, the people who they know, can also affect you.[6] When I reflect on my own life to date, I can recall quite clearly, just a handful of close friends or associates who have inspired me to reach for my highest potential in any given situation. These are people who spread an infectious enthusiasm for enjoyment, creativity, and adventure, at every opportunity. It's not easy to put into words, what the effect of such people can have on you, but the tendency is for you all to bring out the best in one another. It's a feeling of excited and inspired thought and emotion, leading to physical action that can take everyone to new levels of fulfilment through a sort of camaraderie of shared enterprise. It can also put you in a receptive state for what Seth calls, 'the

---

[5] Dr Wayne W. Dyer – 'The Power of Intention'
[6] Research by David Burkus and also work done by Social scientist Dr Nicholas Christakis, at Nuffield College, Oxford and James Fowler, professor of political science at the University of California at San Diego: "friends make you fat."

magical approach.' Conversely, I have also associated with those who have a general 'downer' on life; who complain about the troubles of the world and the lack of opportunity available to them through circumstances beyond their control. This produces feelings of despondency and apathy towards taking action – mental or physical. Try to imagine people in your life who are positive and enthusiastic for life, until you begin to attract them into your physical experience.

Set a realistic goal or target

When I say 'set a realistic goal or target,' this is not meant to diminish your beliefs in miracles or 'help from the universe.' I am simply saying that it benefits you to begin with something you can believe is possible in your current situation. For example, one thing I started to imagine was having £1,000 in my bank account that I wouldn't need to use – something that would provide a cushion for me if an unexpected bill should arise. I felt an instant relief, even just thinking about that. At the time I thought about this, I had no savings and was living precisely within my monthly means. The £1,000 untouched savings didn't happen overnight... but it did happen.

Ask yourself questions before making purchases

When you're shopping, whether in a town or online, start to ask yourself these questions?
- Do I really need this?
- Have I already got something similar?
- Will I actually use it as much as I think?
- When will I use this?
- Am I just bored and looking for something to cheer myself up?
- Do I have anything else that will already fulfil the same purpose or function?
- How will I feel having this?
- How will I feel not having this?
- Would having this also benefit anyone else?

Do not purchase everything immediately. Leave the store. How do you feel now? If you do not feel strongly either way, carry on doing something else. If you feel strong regret or disappointment, perhaps consider returning to make the purchase. Often, leaving a bit of time between finding something, and buying it, is all you need in order to gain a more realistic clarity. Also, don't worry about losing a purchase to someone else. If it's for you, it will still be there when you are ready for it. If you lose it to someone else, how much did it really matter anyway? After a few days you'll probably have forgotten about it anyway.

I once saw a second hand car that I really liked the look of. It was quite unusual, sporty, and in excellent condition. However, it was just before Christmas and I was with family, away from home. I therefore had to wait for about a week before my return home, see if it was still available, give the seller a call, and arrange for a friend to take me to see it. From the outset, I strongly felt inside that it was already mine – but I also let it go. If it was mine, it would wait for me. It did wait... I had a lift to see it, liked it, bought it, set up all the 'legal to drive' stuff, and drove it home, all on the same day.

Do not resent paying your bills

Back in the 1980's, I attended a number of talks and workshops. One of these was given by Australian, Lionel Fifield,[7] who entitled one of his talks: 'Money: Understanding it and ourselves more fully.' Before setting up his Relaxation Centre, he had been an Accountant. Over time, he started to notice the attitudes and behaviours of different clients, when it came to the way they viewed money. Many clients insisted on holding onto their money until the last possible moment an invoice had to be paid; others were fixated on the importance of making lots of money; and some never seemed to make a profit in their businesses. All these variations became very interesting to Lionel.

---

[7] Lionel Fifield – Relaxation Centre of Queensland

Lionel said we should pay our bills with joy and appreciation. These days, we call this 'an attitude of gratitude.' It actually feels great to pay a bill. For one thing, you no longer have to worry about it; and for another, you are forming a good relationship with the person who has provided you with something, such as goods or a service. A personal example of this is when I take my vehicles to my local garage – if I cannot undertake the work myself. I rarely ask them how much something will cost and I always pay them immediately when I collect a vehicle. Because of this, there have been a couple of times when something has gone wrong with a vehicle and I have been able to ask if they could check it for me. Not only do they fit me into their busy day, but sometimes when I ask them "How much?" after they have checked or fixed something, they often say: "Nothing." or "Just remind us to add a half hour's labour next time we do any work for you."

Lionel mentioned a couple of other things that I clearly remember: Money is energy and you want to keep it flowing; and "Go for a walk in your most expensive area and look at all the wonderful houses. Then say: 'I really appreciate looking at all these wonderful houses, where the owners are hardly ever at home to enjoy them, because they are out earning the money to pay for their upkeep – and I have this time to admire them all... and it doesn't cost me a penny!'"

Why do we buy things?

Aside from paying for our food and shelter, many times people buy things to help them to feel better about something else happening in their lives – a sort of distraction. This often works in the short term, but rarely works in the mid to longer term. We have to buy something else to 'make us happy' again. 'Things' can make you happy for a while, but inner joy, peace of mind, or a general sense of wellbeing, support us for much longer and far beyond any material acquisitions. I can remember times in the past when I bought things that gave me a spark of enjoyment and then later, when those things stopped interesting me, or didn't really accomplish what I thought they might, I started feeling stressed at having wasted money I could have saved or used for something different.

The false optimism of sudden financial improvement

This next bit actually ties in with the earlier section on credit cards and loans. As a younger person, with financial hardships, I often managed to increase my borrowing capacity with banks – either through an increase on credit card limits, or slightly bigger loans. In fact, because I was full-time employed, banks would actually raise my credit card limits without me even having to ask. I made the minimum payment every month and when I got close to my limit, and slowed down on using the card, the bank concerned simply raised it to a new, higher limit.

Suddenly having the ability to pay off a few bills, feeling ease at knowing I could pay the next rent on my accommodation, or now being able to buy something I'd had my eye on for a while, also led to a feeling of renewed invincibility. Thoughts like: "I'll be able to do something additional that will make me more money." and "I won't be in this situation again." led to 'throwing caution to the wind,' as the saying goes. The truth was... the money I had managed to procure wasn't really mine. I had to eventually pay it back. But in the euphoria of optimism and removed stress and worry, I hadn't actually done anything to change the situation that got me into my original difficulty. It reminds me of the old proverb: 'Give a man a fish and he will eat for a day. Teach a man how to fish and you feed him for a lifetime.'

It also reminds me of another saying:

'If you give a poor person a lot of money, you haven't now got a rich person; you've just got a poor person with money'.

What this means is, you have not changed the mindset of the person. It's the same person with all their feelings of lack, worry of loss, etc. and in a perverse way, there's almost an inner need to return to the previous comfort level of lack. This is also why another cliché arises:

'The rich get richer and the poor get poorer.'

Well of course they do! You see, it's all about your mental and emotional focus and the beliefs you form as a result. Whatever you concentrate on in your thoughts and actions, brings more of a similar nature. Believe it or not, this is a natural condition of the universe we inhabit. Here are just a few examples of many:

- If you own a particular vehicle, you tend to see more of the same vehicle.
- If you feel distressed by what you see as problems and inequalities in your society, you'll always have a radar detector out for situations and experiences that confirm this belief.
- If you believe that you are poor, you will always find evidence to support this or attract situations where you seem to become poorer. Unexpected expenses; unfair parking fines; increases in costs of living; etc.
- If you believe that people are 'out to take advantage of you,' you'll often come across people who behave in that way, or situations that leave you poorer.

That last point is particularly important, as it says a lot about the way we judge others. In fact, you might say that this booklet is a lot about the judgements we make concerning our relationship to the actions and activities of other people.

Another saying is along the lines of: 'If you leave an area to escape from something, you'll probably find similar issues where you end up.' Once again, if you have not addressed the causes of discomfort, you are quite likely to reproduce them wherever you are... because wherever you go, you are still there. This is one reason why I once left a place, and then returned to it a few years later. I made peace with a place I had felt some upset. As a consequence, I can now stay or go, without the causes of my feelings affecting my next location of choice.

Equality versus equal opportunity

Like many words we use in our societies, some can be misunderstood or put down to semantic[8] subtleties. In this example of equality and equal opportunity, one is about 'being equal' and the other is about 'having access to the same opportunities as others.' If you aspire to circumstances beyond your current situation, and normally 'blame' your lack of equality or equal opportunity on other people or circumstances, do not begrudge those other people who seem to have those things you wish to also have. Instead, be

---

[8] Semantics: Of or relating to meaning or the study of meaning; the study of language meaning; the meaning of a word, phrase or sentence.

grateful that there are people who can demonstrate to you, possibilities you can aspire to. We can all feel stuck by circumstances we feel overwhelmed by, but a good friend of mine once said:

> *"If you can't change your situation, change your attitude."*

This was typical of her down to earth approach to life, but metaphysically, it has a lot of merit. By seeing something differently to the way it appears, and choosing either to not be affected by it, or to be affected by it in a more positive way, you take control of feeling better and allow new energy to improve any situation.

Bashar[9] puts it this way:

> *"Circumstances don't matter. Only state of being matters."*

In his Manifestors Café, Andy Dooley[10] suggested a slight change to this:

> *"Circumstances don't matter. Only **my** state of being matters."*

---

[9] Op. Cit. Bashar
[10] Andy Dooley, Co-founder of TUT.COM and creator of The Manifestor's Cafe

The difference between 'haves' and 'have-nots'

Many people who are experiencing financial difficulty, often feel that if anyone offers to pay for something for them, or actually gives them something for free, there must be a catch or a future pay-back expected – either in money or in kind. I remember, as a young adult, being concerned if I went with more than a couple of friends for a drink at a bar and someone started buying rounds. I won't go into the details of potential unfairness, but suffice to say, it could quickly become either very expensive, or very embarrassing if you couldn't join in. There used to be an expression used by the confident poor: "I'll go Dutch." meaning, I'll pay my own way – in this case, buy my own drinks and not be part of the group rounds.

On the other hand, if a person offering something is genuinely feeling abundant, then actually, he/she/they probably have more than enough left of what they are offering you. To put it another way, a $100 to you may feel like $10 to them. I am speaking from experience here, having been in both situations. Indeed, it once showed up in a very stark example:

One time, I was walking around a town with a friend. Very soon, it was lunchtime and I was feeling quite hungry. "Do you fancy some lunch at that café?" I asked, pointing to a place nearby.

"Okay." she replied. However, on looking at the menu, it was obvious that she was hesitating on ordering. "It's very expensive." she exclaimed. "Don't worry." I replied. "I'll pay." To my surprise, this didn't seem to register and once again, she mentioned the prices. Once again, I said it was fine – I had plenty of money. "Tell you what..." she started. "I know a place that sells excellent sandwiches. We could have one of those and come back here for coffee." With slight reluctance, I gave up and agreed to follow her. We bought our sandwiches, but couldn't stay inside to eat them. In fact, there wasn't really anywhere pleasant to sit, so we ended up standing in a side street, eating our food in the cold, with people passing around us. Not exactly the relaxed lunch and conversation I'd envisaged.

What particularly interested me about that experience was that my friend was transferring her own anxiety of cost onto me. Due to her mindset, there was nothing I could have said that would have reassured her that all was well. Her strength of belief in lack was so strong that she could no longer accept a gift of abundance. It reminded me of this old saying:

You can lead a horse to water – but you cannot make it drink

Never a lender or a borrower be

This is an old wise-saying passed down through generations. When someone lends money, the natural assumption is that they expect repayment at some time in the future. When someone borrows money, they worry about the day they will have to pay it back. The problem here is that both parties are psychologically joined together and effectively held to ransom by their actions of either lending or borrowing and the ensuing worry: One keeps wondering when they'll get their money back; the other keeps worrying about when they can afford to pay it back. So here is a personal decision I made concerning money:

Never borrow and never lend – only give or freely receive.

This translates as only accepting money earned by agreement, or freely given, and never lending money to others, but rather, giving freely with no strings attached. A by-product of this decision has been that not only do I feel great warmth and pleasure in giving, but I also receive more frequently from unexpected sources.

Passive income

Passive income is a situation whereby you set up something that brings you a regular income, but needs very little input to maintain it. Initially, this may require varying amounts of work on your part, but you could, for example, provide some sort of service where a client then continues to 'retain' your expertise for when they need it. Obviously, having control over your own ideas is best, but there are also conventional sales opportunities, when a company or franchise recruits resellers on a non-contractual basis, for promoting and selling its products.

Bear in mind that some resellers will offer training, but then may require a 'buy-in' to products. I would probably avoid these, until you have more experience in knowing you can handle what is required. For instance, you might get all fired up and excited, only to discover that what you have taken on, involves either knowing a lot of friends, or requiring particular 'cold calling' social skills you do not have, or wish to develop. If you take the multi-level marketing route, you probably want to find something where the sale of an existing and popular service does not tie you into a commitment but instead, gains you a small commission on one or more sales. Many such companies encourage team creation and anyone else, who joins, traced back to your recommendation, also gains a commission on sales or introductions to others. As a by-product, this may provide you with an additional commission direct from the main company or franchiser, when your recommendation results in further sales.

Depending on where you are in the world, typical services can include utility and mobile phone companies, but there are many different commercial enterprises that increase their revenue and market share by offering something to participating members of the general public. This way, you are not paying out for products or having to hold stock and you are not forced to engage any more than you feel comfortable doing. We are talking here about ease – not more stress in your life.

If you are good with social media, and have developed a massive following, you might consider becoming an 'influencer.' Companies often look out for people with large followings and offer products that the influencer can promote for a commission.

The aim is to create multiple income streams of *any size*. If you do something whereby ten people are giving you 10 or 20 [of whatever your currency is] every month, this soon adds up to additional income you can use to improve your circumstances. Take it from me, when you have been struggling to survive on not very much, a little extra can feel like quite a big deal. Furthermore, when you begin to see regular money coming in, you get a good feeling inside and you start to expect more opportunities to feed your pond, so to speak.

A few ideas for creating passive income with minimal outlay:

- Offer a service that helps others. Do you have a skill or knowledge that someone would pay for, at regular intervals?
- Can you easily and cheaply make something that could be sold through an online shop – or even your own website shop?
- Are you good with social media? Could you gain a following and then market something related to your interests?
- Depending on interests and abilities, are there any other online sites that you could create things for and gain income? For example, 'bandcamp' for musicians, where people can download single tracks or albums; or Amazon Kindle for writers of e-books.
- Could you learn to create mobile device websites? You can charge a fee for creation and afterwards, negotiate a monthly maintenance fee to include adding or amending items.
- Could you offer online consultancy on something?

Remember, you are aiming to do something which is easy and gives you pleasure. You do not want to take on additional expenses, so this may put some limitations on what you choose to pursue, but you do want to start receiving extra income. The excitement of this approach is that you never quite know what you are going to receive or when you are going to receive it. The bottom line is: It doesn't matter. This is a good attitude to have. Call it a sort of surrender to non-attachment. Set up enough of these, little income stream, ideas and you'll soon find that a constant drip-feed becomes a healthy flow to your pond of abundance.

Selling your service and deciding on cost

This is an area that a lot of people worry about. There are a few ways you can view this:

1. What does it cost me to provide this [whatever it is] for someone?
2. What do other people charge for the same, or similar, item or service?
3. How much will materials cost?
4. How much will gas, electricity, or other fuel cost – for production or heating?
5. What price do I put on my time?
6. What price do I put on my knowledge and expertise?
7. Do I want a specific amount for my services, or will I enjoy this so much, that I'd either do it for nothing, or accept any amount of monetary contribution?

If you are running your own business, you will probably already have a good idea about where you stand on the first six points. However, if you are simply wishing to attract a bit of extra income, the last point may feel more comfortable for you.

An example, from my own life, has been building websites. For a while, I tried to use the rational approach and to come up with a range of fixed pricing options. But, in the end, this became too complicated. There are so many levels of complexity with web work, so, in the end, it was easier to decide on a minimum amount and work up from there. For example, asking a client about the nature of their website ambitions and any specific requirements they needed, which might make the 'basic' level of work more complex. From experience, I often knew what might be involved and could build an appropriate quote from my base level, upwards. However, there have also been occasions when I have offered some free help – and this is where things become interesting.

When you answer a call for help from others, and offer to assist with an open heart, without any expectation to receive, you'll often find that the universe gets behind both yourself, and the person you are helping. Furthermore, when it comes to any offer of remuneration, it's safe to suggest: "Whatever you feel able to offer." Okay, a certain level of trust, and faith in the divine, is required here, but if you were able to help with joy, you've already received one reward. Whatever you are offered on top, is going to be a bonus. And what's more, when you do not set an expectation too high, not only do you often receive more than you might have asked for, but the person giving to you also feels comfortable with their offer. It's a win-win situation!

Further techniques

Can you locate the source of the feeling you have surrounding money? Very often, when you think about something that causes you stress or upset, you get feelings in certain areas of the body. For example: a feeling of anxiety in the stomach area.

Also, try to visualize the area of your brain where concerns or blocks might be around finances. Here's one of my own examples:

The funnel of money

I had a feeling, like as if there was a funnel, just above my head, full of gold coins. It seemed to symbolise the abundance that was already waiting for me and all I had to do was let it in – or in the case of the funnel, let it out. The trouble was, it was an old rusty funnel and there seemed to be a cork stuck in the bottom, stopping the coins from escaping. Every night, just after I'd gone to bed, I'd lay there with this vision – trying to reach the cork to convincingly remove it. I say convincingly, because part of me was not accepting that removing the cork would really free up my abundance and sometimes the cork would be slightly dislodged, only to return to its fitted position the following night. Gradually, I managed to dislodge the cork and one night, it was no longer there. However, the tube from the funnel was too narrow for the coins to flow. What else could I do?

I pretended to look inside my brain. Perhaps I could locate something in the physical workings of my mind. I imagined synaptic pathways with sparks of flashing light, as thoughts travelled around, connecting information that allowed me to function. It was like looking through a forest of interconnecting fibres – some fine, some thicker. Suddenly, I noticed something dark and thick, like a tree root, coming down from the top of my head and twisting to the right. It seemed to terminate at a dead end and its flow of energy had all but ceased. The density had almost no light. I instinctively knew that this was the cause of my mental difficulty. For the next few nights, I imagined hacking away at the root, trying to cut off its supply of negativity. Eventually, it began to wilt and I was able to reconnect it to what I thought might be a more helpful location. The energy was now flowing in a more positive way and the sparks of light had returned.

A deep dive into metaphysics

I am now going to take you into a deep dive – into the world of metaphysics. Some of what follows may seem complex and you do not have to understand it all; it is however, included here as general reference material to refer back to, whenever you are ready for it.

Brain and Mind

There is a common misconception about where the mind is located. Science of course says it is integral to the physical brain, but to use a cliché, that is a very narrow-minded conclusion. Science might then say that they can measure brainwave activity in the brain and that proves the mind is there. Furthermore, it concludes that the only consciousness that exists in a body is contained within the body. Fine if mind were only a physical attribute of the body, rather than non-physical consciousness interfacing with the body. Metaphysically speaking, your physical brain allows you to interpret your experience of physical reality – otherwise, simply put; nothing would make sense in our physical experience. Consciousness interfaces with the physical organism and some of the action of that interfacing can be viewed using physical monitoring equipment. This does not mean that the mind is being viewed; it simply means that the action of the mind consciousness, through the physical body, can be witnessed and measured in a particular way, showing how it variously connects around the body. Seth calls our physical reality 'camouflage' and says:

"Your scientists' instruments are themselves distortive, and will only allow you to probe further into camouflage. What you need are tools and instruments that are free from camouflage."[11]

I suggest that your mind is ubiquitous; it is everywhere and has connections beyond anywhere you can imagine. Indeed, even science, through quantum physics, has begun to realise that everything in the universe appears to be connected. Your true non-physical self, or your inviolate [indestructible] soul, if you like, is beyond

---

[11] Seth, The Early Sessions 2, Session 49 April 29, 1964 Also: "Scientists realize that the atmosphere of the earth has a distorting effect upon their instruments. What they do not understand is that their instruments themselves are bound to be distortive. Any material instrument will have built-in distortive effects. The one instrument which is more important than any other is the mind (not the brain) . . . the meeting place of the inner and outer senses. The mind is distributed throughout the entire physical body and builds up about it the physical camouflage necessary for existence on the physical level. The mind receives data from the inner senses and forms the necessary camouflage. The brain deals exclusively with camouflage patterns, while the mind deals with basic principles inherent on all planes. The brain is, itself, part of the camouflage pattern and can be interpreted and probed by physical instruments. The mind cannot. The mind is the connective. It is here that the secrets of the universe will be discovered, and the mind itself is the tool of discovery. You might say that the brain is the mind in camouflage."

your human, five senses comprehension. But don't worry, that doesn't matter for now. Essentially, you channel yourself into and through your physical body – 'spirit made manifest through flesh' so to speak. However, you also send information back to non-physical, from the physical experience.

It might be worth adding an aside here, that the physical body is terminated and re-created many millions of times a second.[12] If this is indeed the case, and given that physicists admit that as you zoom into finer and finer levels of detail, everything is just movement and nothing is actually solid, then it seems that there would be no way to preserve conscious continuity, if it resided only in the physical brain. Therefore, surely it must stream into the body from elsewhere. Seth touches on this in one of what he calls, 'The Three Dilemmas':

"It is this dilemma, precisely between identity's constant attempts to maintain stability, and action's inherent drive for change, that results in the imbalance, the exquisite creative by-product that is consciousness of <u>self</u>. We have a series of creative <u>strains</u>. Identity must seek stability while action must seek change, yet identity could not exist without change, without action, for it is the

---

[12] Seth mentions this in several places, but most notably in 'The Three Creative Dilemmas'. (The Early Sessions 3, Session 138 March 8, 1965).

result of action, and not apart from it but a part of it."[13]

In simpler terms, our identity of self wants to remain safe and constant, but everything it attempts to attach to, wants change; and as regards our consciousness, maybe think of the mind consciousness in the physical brain, similar to the RAM[14] in a computer, and the non-physical source of your consciousness like the ROM[15] in a computer. RAM is volatile memory that temporarily stores the files you are working with. ROM is non-volatile memory that permanently stores instructions for your computer. When you disconnect power from your computer, the RAM is cleared. When you switch on your computer, it reloads its essential information from the ROM. Scale this up to great speed and remove ideas of linear time, and your 'moment point'[16] is a whole lifetime.

---

[13] Op. Cit. Seth, footnote 6
[14] Random Access Memory
[15] Read Only Memory
[16] "The moment point is in itself arbitrary, an artificial division. [...] the moment point for you is actually composed of the amount of action which you are capable of assimilating within your present framework, for the moment point is indeed a portion of the spacious present." – The Early Sessions 4, Session 151 May 3, 1965

"In actuality there is only a spacious present, so spacious that it cannot be explored all at once in your terms, hence your arbitrary division of it into larger rooms of past, present and future." – TES1 Session 41 April 6, 1964

A two-way highway

Scientifically, all information is contained within the individual and the responses to environment, experiential daily situations and circumstances, reside purely within the physical mind and body. If you have a problem, you work it out in the mind, rationally, logically, or emotionally. You do this based on what you think you know and sometimes with help from others who may know more than you.

Metaphysically, from your physical earthly standpoint, you react to experiences you perceive that you are in. I say 'perceive' because very often, the experience you think you are having may not be the experience that is really happening. Furthermore, *"You create your own reality"*[17] and the environment and circumstances you then experience are purely physical feedback to what you are creating from within your true selfhood. Let me put a version of this in its own paragraph. Please read it a few times until you get it:

What you see around you, in your every moment, is physical feedback created from the inner environment you are electromagnetically projecting outwards

---

[17] Seth, The Early Class Sessions 1, ESP Class Session, April 22, 1969 (but also mentioned in other sessions)

which manifests symbolically into mirrored physical forms
of your overall mental and psychic state

Most people believe the world is 'out there' and coming at them. They react to the physical feedback as if it were totally independent of them. Before we continue, let's introduce you to a couple of Seth's 'Frameworks': Framework 1 (physical reality) and Framework 2 (non-physical reality). I'm going to keep things simple. The first is where we have our physical, earthly experience; the second is non-physical, a much more expansive and knowledgeable environment where all things available to us are known. Furthermore, linear time, as we have come to accept it in physical reality, does not apply in non-physical reality. Everything is simultaneous and there are no divisions of past, present, or future – only a 'spacious present'.[18]

So what about this two-way highway? When you respond to something physically, you most often respond first mentally and emotionally. Some reactions are instant and automatic without thinking, often exemplified in some situations by the famous psychological expression: 'fight or flight.' Most of the functions of our body are not

---

[18] *"In actuality there is only a spacious present, so spacious that it cannot be explored all at once in your terms, hence your arbitrary division of it into larger rooms of past, present and future."* - Seth, The Early Sessions 1, Session 41 April 6, 1964

consciously controlled by us and we often call these autonomic. Responses such as 'fight or flight' are often explained by Science and psychology as originating from the earliest times of our brain's development [anthropologically and evolutionarily speaking] when humanoids were developing their understanding of the physical domain – our world, the Earth – when basic survival from death was paramount. Sometimes referred to as 'the reptilian brain'; also referred to as the amygdale – the area of the brain where medical science says we store, among other things, trauma from shocking experiences we struggled to cope with.

But trauma and fear does not have to be attached only to an immediate physical event. We have creative thoughts and memories of numerous experiences and encounters with other people and events that cause us to be on our guard. Effectively, we are sending signals to the body of concern for our safety or wellbeing, even when nothing is physically endangering us. Let me put it the Mark Twain way:

"I've had a lot of worries in my life, most of which never happened."

What metaphysics also says is that we send these emotional messages into Framework 2, where answers or solutions are immediately formed to help us, back in Framework 1. However, if we send a 'false' message of alert – in other words, we have misinterpreted or exaggerated our situation – then the feedback we receive may feel unhelpful to the real situation we find ourselves in, or simply get blocked by our rational and panicking thoughts, holding us in a state of perpetually heightened alert. We are, in a sense, putting ourselves into a position of 'fight or flight' when nothing is immediately threatening us. People, who are constantly worried about their financial circumstances, are often in a permanent state of exaggerated fear for what could happen to them.

Back to money and finances

So, what has any of this got to do with money and our finances? When you worry about money to the level of anxiety, the message sent to Framework 2 is not interpreted as requesting the opposite but rather, a request for more of the same. I'm sure you have come across this expression: 'energy flows where attention goes.' As we grow up in our world, from infant to adult, those before us often say, 'in order to solve a problem you must focus attention on it.' Indeed, much of our education revolves around focusing attention on risk assessments – before we even attempt to do anything! However, metaphysically speaking, when you focus on a problem, you add to the energy strength of the problem. This is why many people now say: 'focus on solutions.' This automatically puts you in a different mindset. You are now thinking about what you would prefer in your experience, rather than focusing on the experience you have, up to this moment, created. Exploring solutions activates images of possible desired outcomes, rather than embedding yourself in thoughts about insurmountable problems.

Abraham[19] often tells us:

"You cannot turn your attention to a problem without shining your attention on it, activating the vibration within you. Every thought is already vibrating, so when you focus on it you activate the vibration of it within you. If you stay focused there for as little as 17 seconds, it becomes a point of attraction that begins to expand.

"After 68 seconds, a thought so active, is a belief.

"Thoughts that you just think – they are just thoughts. Thoughts you keep thinking become chronically thought – easier to think. Those are what beliefs are. Those represent your expectation and once you've reached expectation, things start showing up in your experience. Now you've got proof, now you don't just believe it, you know it! You expect it. You expect it to be the way that it is."

---

[19] Op. Cit. Abraham-Hicks

I know for some, it will seem a bit far-fetched talking about these metaphysical subjects, in what seems to be an otherwise rational subject of needing more financial abundance in their lives. However, you may as well have as much information as possible. Pick the tools which you can work with and maybe try a few of the others along the way.

One of the things Seth tells us, is that when we first try to change a long standing pattern of behaviour, for a while there is a sort of, what I sometimes term, 'energy catch-up,' with a mismatch of where we have been, with where we are heading. It might also be worth mentioning here, that what you think of as your 'present' in some ways, is your past made manifest in the present. Your thoughts and actions, up to this moment, have created what you are now experiencing. Seth puts it this way:

"To change the physical effect you must change the original belief – while being quite aware that for a time physical materialization of the old beliefs may still hold. If you completely understand what I am saying however, your new beliefs will – and quickly – begin to show themselves in your experience. But you must not be concerned for their emergence, for this brings up the fear that the new ideas will not materialize and so this negates your purpose." – Seth[20]

---

[20] The Nature of Personal Reality: Session 621 Oct 16 1972 9.40pm Monday

I experienced this energy catch-up when I had a protracted spell of sciatica[21] which was by now into its 7th month. I wasn't initially sure how I came to have this, but gradually realised, that for about a year I had felt that my home was getting too cluttered and that it was becoming difficult to enjoy any restful spaces. Psychologically, my thoughts about this lack of space were weighing heavily on my sense of wellbeing – it was becoming difficult to move around without something being in the way. I had a music studio set up at one side of the lounge and my couch and armchairs were being pushed closer and closer to the wall and a television on the opposite side of the room. Eventually, with the encouragement of a friend – also going through similar feelings and a resulting de-cluttering exercise – I spent a week clearing and reorganising the room as well as some other areas in the house – taking several car loads to charity/thrift shops, the local recycle, and offering some things free to friends. With the main room now clear of its blocked energy, and returned to a more spacious, fit for purpose lounge, it immediately felt more relaxing. However, despite the physical changes, it took almost 2 more weeks before the effects of the new energy in the room really changed – from the way it had been to the way it now appeared... and then my sciatica vanished.

---

[21] Sciatica – described as neuralgia or acute spasmodic pain along the sciatic nerve

There are many instances when your environment is clearly a symbolic representation of your state of inner wellbeing and the physical feedback can give you clues to the things you need to change – whether those be thoughts, or practices.

So be aware that many of your manifested financial difficulties can relate to how you feel about different aspects of your mental and emotional life. A change in the way you feel about your self inside, has to be reflected in a physical change externally – resulting in a change in the physical feedback you then begin to witness.

Common inner causes of outward poverty include some of the following:

- Not feeling worthy to receive.
- Not feeling 'good enough' in general terms.
- Not feeling that you can have certain things.
- Experiencing past rejection when you asked for financial or emotional support.
- Feeling that it may not be your destiny to have money.
- Feeling that you cannot charge others for your work or services.
- Thinking that if you charge above a certain amount, you will lose potential clients.
- Falsely believing that your abilities are not as good as other people.
- Feeling that having a lot of money may turn you into a nasty person.

- Believing that there may not be enough to go around.
- Believing that if you have more, others will have less.

The choice to feel different

One thing that Abraham[22] suggests to us, when we find our attention constantly moving towards worry and concern, is:

"Try and reach for the better feeling thought."

So in a way, you might say we choose to be happy or sad. Of course, it doesn't feel that way when our mind spirals down the rabbit hole of despair. It seems so easy to link one negative thought to another. Before long, we are so deep into our worry that we are completely unaware of anything else. If for just one minute, we could turn our attention to a happier thought and produce a happier emotional feeling, we would break that chain of despair.

In my own experience, focusing on a better feeling thought was not easy at first. However, I did find that with a bit of practice I could simply look around myself and notice something in my immediate environment that would distract me from my despondency. All you have to do is break

---

[22] Op. Cit. Abraham-Hicks

the connection – no matter how briefly. Go and do something to take your mind off the worry; watch some comedy on TV or YouTube; read a book; make yourself a hot drink.

Seth tells us we can always change anything for the better:

"Feel and dwell upon the certainty that your emotional, spiritual and psychic abilities are focused through the flesh, and for five minutes only direct all of your attention toward what you want. Use visualization or verbal thought—whatever comes most naturally to you; but for that period do not concentrate upon any lacks, just upon your desire."[23]

You could also try writing down on paper, a positive scenario, opposite to your current situation. This is sometimes called 'scripting' and it works brilliantly to focus your attention, instead of just thinking in your head and getting distracted. (Some people also speak of 'journaling' but to me, this is more like keeping a diary, rather than projecting ahead).

Do not check for change

Seth goes on to say:

---

[23] Seth – The Nature of Personal Reality, Session 657

"Use all of your energy and attention. <u>Then</u> forget about it. Do not check to see how well it is working. Simply make sure that in that period your intentions are clear. Then in one way or another, according to your own individual situation, make one physical gesture or act that is in line with your belief or desire. Behave physically, then, at least once a day in a way that shows that you have faith in what you are doing."[24]

(Remember the example of leaving money on the table?)

I'm sure this is another difficult thing for many people: wondering whether their actions and activities are starting to bear fruit. It's like the proverbial gardener digging up the ground to see if the seeds planted a few days before have started sprouting. It's the same with your finances. Furthermore, by checking on progress and seeing no change, you start focusing on failure and reinforcing your feelings of lack. However, I would add this: If you naturally notice a positive change, no matter how small, celebrate it and build on it in your imagination – you could even write a thank you letter to the universe, acknowledging what you have noticed and expressing a desire for more. Feel gratitude for any improvement, no matter how small.

---

[24] Op. Cit. Seth – The Nature of Personal Reality, Session 657

You live in a physical reality – give it time

Rationally, and metaphysically, we share a physical experience within what I call, 'a bubble of linear time'. This may seem to contradict the notion that there is no real physical reality or time and everything is some sort of psychological illusion of non-physical reality in a spacious present... but since we are here, we need to appreciate something. I'll let Seth say it, since he is always succinct and to the point:

"When you try to change your convictions in order to change your experience, you also have to first stop the momentum that you have already built up, so to speak. You are changing the messages while the body is used to reacting smoothly, unquestioningly, to a certain set of beliefs.

"There is a steady even flow in which conscious activity through the neurological structure brings about events, and a familiar pattern of reaction is established. When you alter these conscious beliefs through effort, then a period of time is necessary while the structure learns to adjust to the new preferred situation.

"If beliefs are changed overnight, comparatively less time is required."[25]

---
[25] Seth, The Nature of Personal Reality, Session 656.

Bashar[26] tells us not to be lazy when we recognise we are caught in habitual behaviour:

"A habit once identified and done again is not a habit – it's a choice."

New Habits

Humans are generally quite habitual. Some part of us not only likes the stability of routine, but also becomes tram-lined into it. We also, as generally social beings, have a tendency to follow the herd and not take our own paths. Furthermore, we look for acceptance from others – social media being a prime example – and we want to feel we are 'on the right track.' Over the past few years, I've been very interested in noticing my own routines and habits and it's been a fascinating exercise of laziness, reluctance, and salvation. Let me give an example:

Eating sweets (candy) after an evening meal. On one occasion, you are determined that you will not have the sweets and right up to the time you are actually eating your meal, you feel no compulsion or desire to have sweets afterwards. However, as soon as you finish, you suddenly feel like a sweet. The subtlety of this is timed to the second. Even though you made a decision prior to the habit

---

[26] Bashar is a member of an off-world alien race, channelled by Darryl Anka

kicking in, you still felt compelled to succumb at the last moment.

Habits can be associative and/or relational. For example: the pattern of routines leading up to the meal, or the location of where you are having the meal. Simply by visiting a friend's house and eating an evening meal there, does not invoke the desire for sweets afterwards – because you do not associate the behaviour with visiting your friend's location, or eating there. Removed from context, there is nothing to trigger any of your usual home-based responses.

Similarly, you have habitual behaviour associated with the way you respond to your financial situation. In all likelihood the emotional responses of worry will be stronger than those of the desire for sweets, so the strength of energy is more highly charged. What you can try is refocusing that energy onto something more helpful. Here are a couple of ideas:

The first is something that Esther Hicks[27] did. Get a piece of paper and draw a line down the centre. On the left side title it: 'What I can do.' On the right side title it: 'What I will leave the universe to take care of.' Now write a few things under each of those headings. By giving over something to the universe, you can let go and relax a bit – you don't need to

---

[27] Esther Hicks 'interprets' the Abraham information.

concern yourself with this now. It's being taken care of.

Another thing you may experience when worrying, is keeping yourself awake at night, trying to work everything out. A good way to stop this is to write things down on paper – particularly if you are worried you might forget something. Once this is done, you can sleep, knowing that you have your note to refer back to in the morning. In other words, park the worry on the paper.

The second is an ancient reconciliation practice from Hawaii called Ho'oponopono.[28] I have used this many times and continue to do so. Simply feel your emotions surrounding any subject and keep repeating, inside yourself:

I love you
I'm sorry
Please forgive me
Thank you

You can say those in any order. Sometimes it may be easier to start with 'I'm sorry'. As you repeat the mantra, other worries or upsets may come to the surface. Keep going until you naturally come to a stop.

---

[28] Ho'oponopono (ho-o-pono-pono) is an ancient Hawaiian practice of reconciliation and forgiveness which literally means, to "make right". You can read more on my website here: keekoo.co.uk/hooponopono

The essence of this mantra[29] is based on the fact that you create your own reality and take full responsibility for your actions and subsequent experiences. Not only are you loving your self, and apologising for creating these situations in your physical feedback, but you are also sending out love to the situation, followed by thanks, in anticipation of a resolution. A question that goes with this mantra is:

What is going on in me that I am obtaining this experience?

The question is based on the premise that for something to show up in your external experience there must be something inside of you that has become strong enough, in its focus of energy, to manifest some physical feedback that you are now experiencing. To change the experience (unless you like it) you must change the internal thoughts and feelings. Reciting the mantra seems to play a part in making this change and it often comes in positive ways – often surprisingly quickly.

Lastly, I would suggest not getting cross with yourself for having a habit. In my experience, accepting a habit, together with expressing the desire for a change away from the habit, is enough to let things run their course and disappear. It really

---

[29] Mantra - A Sanskrit term loosely described as meaning a sound, word, or phrase that is repeated – used as an instrument of thought (although some other definitions are also given, such as: "instrument of thought")

is the same for most things: the more you think about something, the more energy you feed into it, and the more life you give it. Once the strength of thought and focus is removed, the emotion dissolves or dissipates into weaker elements. The important thing in this example is to express a preference for something different.

Some say that forming new habits can take at least a month of daily repetition – sometimes up to 90 days. Try not to treat change like having a sandwich toaster. You get this device and for a couple of weeks, you make hot sandwiches every day. One day, you put it away in the cupboard and forget about it. A year or two later, you suddenly find it in the cupboard and wonder why you stopped using it. It's as if something in our mind gently whispers: "Right, you've been there and done that now – moving on!" This tendency to flit from one thing to another is perhaps a bi-product of modern living. We seem to inhabit a world of short attention spans, where a lack of immediate success in one area, sends us towards seeking new gratification, or faster results, from another. For example, a common tendency in the metaphysical/spiritual community is to go from one teacher or training course to another: coming away feeling inspired and invigorated... and then not actually applying what we have learnt. Suddenly it's all too much effort. The feedback rewards are illusive and, before too long, we're off looking for someone, or something else, to solve all our problems and fulfil our desires more quickly – so be mindful this!

Intention

You may recall that earlier on, I mentioned an intention to pay bills or pay back debts, regardless of current ability to do so. Now I am going to look at the power of intention more closely.

In my original 1987 booklet, 'How We Perform Negative Miracles,' I listed a number of words that I felt had some of the most powerful and transformative actions behind them. One of these words was 'intention.' Later, in 2004, Dr Wayne Dyer devoted a whole book to it called 'The Power of Intention.' But without becoming too deep and complex, let me share what I have found to be important about intention. The clue is in the word – intent. When you intend to do something, you usually have a motive in mind to take some sort of action. Take for example, swatting a fly or letting a fly out. The intent behind the action is different in both cases. In the first, the intent is to kill; in the second the intent is to help. The same goes for any intention you have, in order to accomplish something. When you harness the power of intent, through emotion, you will feel it propelling you towards some sort of action; you will often find that your motivation increases to bring about a desired end result.

Expectation

This is another powerful word. When you have a strong inner expectation that something is going to definitely happen, the energy to bring that event or outcome into physical expression, becomes much stronger. It's as if, whatever you are expecting has already happened. For example, when you order something online, you expect it to arrive by the duly promised delivery date. You generally do not order something and then immediately worry about whether or not it will arrive.

The magical approach

This was the title used for one of the Jane Roberts' Seth books. Seth gives this definition:

"I want it understood that we are indeed dealing with two entirely different approaches to reality and to solving problems — methods we will here call the rational method and the magical one. The rational approach works quite well in certain situations, such as mass production of goods, or in certain kinds of scientific measurements — but all in all the rational method, as it is understood and used, does not work as an overall approach to life, or in the solving of problems that involve

subjective rather than objective measurements or calculations."[30]

In a discussion with Jane's husband, Rob, regarding some of Jane's health issues, Seth offers an insight that also, in more general terms, broadly applies to all of us:

"Ruburt[31] *feels hopeless at times because the assumptions of the rational approach often lead in that direction, and because he has not been certain enough of himself in those other areas to get the kind of long-lasting results he wants. This applies to both of your attitudes at times.*

"At a conscious level, of course, neither of you realized, or wanted to realize, the kind of complete repeal and overhaul that was implied by our sessions, and for some years you managed to hold many official views of reality along with the newer concepts, not ready to understand that an entire new way of thinking was involved, a new relationship of the individual with reality. So you tried out some new methods piecemeal, here and there, with good-enough results.

"Of course, an entire <u>reorientation</u> (with emphasis) is instead implied, and that entire reorientation will effortlessly bring about a new relationship of

---

[30] Seth – TMA Session One August 6, 1980

[31] Seth refers to Jane as Ruburt and Rob as Joseph – names that most fit with who their personalities are to Seth

Ruburt with his body, with his life, and with the adventure the two of you have embarked upon. He will simply automatically get better, <u>because the framework will allow him to do so</u>."[32]

Surrender

This is a term you may have come across, thought you understood, to varying degrees, but then wondered what on earth it means. It's connected to the "entire reorientation" that Seth mentioned, above. It's a letting go of rational control over situations you simply cannot hope to control. It's giving over your control to something greater than your self. It's not always a surrender of failure and weakness; it's simply an inner acknowledgement that you recognise a greater universal force available to you – and you are fully cooperating to trust it. Think of that first 'Star Wars' film, when Obi-Wan Kenobi uses his mind to communicate to Luke Skywalker in the X-wing Starfighter, on his final attempt to destroy the Death Star weapon: "Use the force Luke." Luke throws aside the electronic computer guidance system, lets go and surrenders, and simply allows the force to work through him, in choosing the right moment to fire and win the battle. Surrender takes faith. You have to let go and simply trust that everything will work out for you, without further rational intervention on your part. This is when miracles happen.

---

[32] Seth – TMA Session Four August 18, 1980

And then it was gone

There will come a time when your financial blocks to more fiscal abundance will begin to dissolve and your situation, whatever it has been, improves – and interestingly, you may not notice when that transition occurs. The motion of universal energy is seamless and subtle. However, what you will notice is the bigger, unexpected positive things that happen. You may for instance start to find that you receive larger amounts of money than you were expecting and some of these will appear from unexpected or previously unconsidered sources. I'm not necessarily talking about thousands at this point, but let's say you had expected £10 and received instead, £100. That's surely a win! Further on, you will start to notice that every time you pay out money, without any concern, it quickly returns. This is the magical approach in action. The final thing that happens, is that you suddenly realise you have stopped thinking about money. You buy, sell, give, receive; like a tide on a calm sunny day, moving gently in and out of a bay, unimpeded by the friction of sand and rocks – simply moving around obstacles and back again. It's unlikely that you will be able to explain this change in your life to others, and trying to use conventional words and descriptions will not cover it. Now you have reached a place of true, natural abundance. Now you can get on with your life. Now you can focus on the things that bring you feelings of joy.

www.ingramcontent.com/pod-product-compliance
Lightning Source LLC
Chambersburg PA
CBHW012000090526
44591CB00018B/2717